Tree Homes

Carol Ghiglieri

SCHOLASTIC INC.

NEW YORK • TORONTO • LONDON • AUCKLAND • SYDNEY
MEXICO CITY • NEW DELHI • HONG KONG • BUENOS AIRES

ISBN-13: 978-0-545-00713-9 / ISBN-10: 0-545-00713-5

Photos Credits:
Cover © Joe McDonald/Corbis; title page: © Rob Reijnen/Foto Natura/Minden Pictures; contents page, from top: © Leonard Lee Rue III/Earth Scenes/Animals Animals, © Kim Taylor/Nature Picture Library, © John Cancalosi/Nature Picture Library; page 4: © Leonard Lee Rue III/Earth Scenes/Animals Animals; page 5: © Bruce Lichtenberger/Peter Arnold Inc.; page 6: © Mike Wilkes/Nature Picture Library; page 7: © Stephen Dalton/Minden Pictures; page 8: © Kim Taylor/Nature Picture Library; page 9: © Lightscapes Photography Inc./Corbis; page 10: © Jason Edwards/Getty Images; page 11: © Bates Littlehales/Getty Images; page 12: © John Cancalosi/Nature Picture Library; page 13, top left: © Stephen Dalton/Minden Pictures; page 13, top right: © Rob Reijnen/Foto Natura/Minden Pictures; page 13, bottom left: © Joke Stuurman-Huitema/Foto Natura/Minden Pictures; page 14: © Michael Durham/Minden Pictures; page 14, inset: © Kim Taylor/Nature Picture Library; page 15: © RPM Pictures/Getty Images; page 16: © Hans Reinhard/zefa/Corbis; back cover: © Jacob Taposchaner/Getty Images.

Photo research by Dwayne Howard
Design by Holly Grundon

12 11 10 9 8 7 6 5 4 3 2 1   7 8 9 10 11 12/0

Printed in the U.S.A.
First printing, September 2007

Contents

Chapter 1

Terrific Trees

Trees are terrific! They are pretty to look at. They give us shade. And for many creatures, trees make great homes.

Fast Fact

Raccoons can open garbage cans with their paws.

Look at the raccoon! Raccoons like to live in the **hollows** of trees. They sleep during the day. They hunt for food at night.

Fast Fact

Squirrels love acorns! They bury these nuts in the ground to eat later.

Squirrels live in trees, too. They build their nests high up in the branches. This helps squirrels stay safe.

Fast Fact

Some Squirrels can leap a distance of 10 feet!

Squirrels are excellent tree climbers. They leap from branch to branch like circus **acrobats**!

Chapter 2

Bird Houses

A redwing picks a berry from a tree.

All kinds of birds live in trees. They use their sharp beaks to grab berries, seeds, insects, and worms.

A robin feeds a worm to her babies.

Birds also use their beaks to build nests. They make their nests out of grass, twigs, and even spiderwebs!

barn owl

Owls live in trees. They are **birds of prey**. That means they hunt other animals for food. They munch on mice, lizards, and insects.

Fast Fact

Woodpeckers have very long tongues.

woodpecker

Guess what else lives in trees? Woodpeckers! They peck at tree trunks to reach the insects that live in the bark. Yum! Lunch!

Chapter 3

Snakes, Bugs, and Bats

king snake

Sometimes snakes live in trees. They **coil** themselves around branches like this.

aphid

beetle

gypsy moth

Too many insects can harm a tree.

Trees are also home to a lot of insects. These bugs eat leaves, bark, and **sap**.

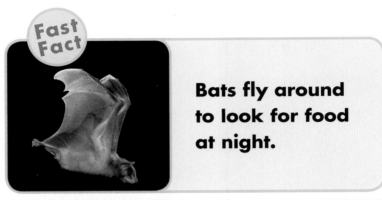

Bats fly around
to look for food
at night.

hoary bat

You might even spot a bat in a tree! This one
is getting ready for a nap.

So the next time you see a tree, remember that it is not only pretty to look at. It is also a home for many amazing animals!

Glossary

acorns (**ay**-kornz): the seeds of an oak tree

acrobats (**ak**-ruh-batz): people at the circus who spin and flip in the air

birds of prey (**burdz** of **pray**): birds that hunt other animals for food

coil (**koil**): to wind around something

hollows (**hol**-ohz): holes or empty spaces in trees

paws (**pawz**): the clawed feet of animals

sap (**sap**): a sticky juice made by trees

Comprehension Questions

1. Can you name two animals with fur that live in trees?

2. Can you name two animals with feathers that live in trees?

3. Can you name two insects that live in trees?